CLAUDE BOLLING
plays *Standards*

CONTENTS

T0056326

ISBN 978-1-4234-8355-7

HAL•LEONARD®
CORPORATION
7777 W. BLUEMOUND RD. P.O. BOX 13819 MILWAUKEE, WI 53213

Visit Hal Leonard Online at
www.halleonard.com

CLAUDE BOLLING
Biography

Pianist, composer, arranger and orchestra conductor Claude Bolling is without a doubt one of the most highly regarded French musicians in the world. Known primarily for his jazz compositions, he also has made contributions to classical, contemporary, television, and film music.

Bolling was born in Cannes, France on April 10, 1930, and has spent most of his life in Paris. It was after his first piano lessons that Claude became passionate about music, learning at an early age that music allowed him to express his artistic sensitivity in creative ways. Through a school friend he discovered the world of jazz, becoming interested in the music of the great jazz pianists Fats Waller, Willie Smith, Earl Hines and Erroll Garner.

During the German Occupation he stayed in Nice where he studied with drummer, pianist and trumpeter Marie-Louise "Bob" Colin. In 1945, at the age of fifteen, Bolling won an amateur musical contest sponsored by Jazz Hot and the Hot Club of France in Paris, creating his own performing group the next year. By the age of eighteen Bolling made his first recording, which led him to pursue a traditional music education. He studied classical piano with Germaine Mounier, jazz piano with Leo Chauliac, harmony with Maurice Duruflé, and counterpoint, orchestration, and jazz composition with André Hodeir.

While serving in the army Bolling was part of the military band Premier Train des Equipages, playing the trombone and percussion. Later he began playing in "à la mode" jazz clubs such as the Club Saint-Germain, the Vieux Colombier, the Caveau de la Huchette and other well-known clubs. During this time he was in great demand by notable American jazz artists on tour in France. He participated in recording sessions and concerts with Rex Stewart, Buck Clayton, Lionel Hampton, Albert Nicholas, and Roy Eldridge, becoming one of the top musicians in the Paris jazz world.

While writing and recording the arrangement of "Chansons Possibles et Impossibles" Bolling met Boris Vian. The success of this recording introduced him to the world of pop music. He produced recordings for many famous artists of the '50s and the '60s, including Sacha Distel, Jacqueline François, Juliette Greco, Henri Salvador, and Brigitte Bardot.

René Clément commissioned him to score the music for *Le Jour et l'Heure*, beginning his career as a film and TV composer. Bolling has written over one hundred scores, some of which have become huge successes, including *Borsalino, Louisiane, Flic Story,*

Le Magnifique, The Awakening, and *California Suite.* In the '60s he worked as the musical director for popular television shows with Albert Raisner, Maritie and Gilbert Carpentier, and Jean-Christophe Averty, writing many memorable tunes, such as "Les Brigades du Tigre," "La Garçonne," and "Le Clan."

Bolling's success and wide-ranging experience enabled him to work with talented musicians in many different genres. He invented a new way of expressing himself, a musical style some referred to as a happy marriage of jazz and classical music. His *Suite for Flute and Jazz Piano Trio* (written for and recorded with Jean-Pierre Rampal) enjoyed a huge success in the United States, staying on the charts for five hundred and thirty weeks, winning gold and platinum records. This led to collaborations with Alexandre Lagoya, Pinchas Zukerman, Maurice André, Yo Yo Ma, the English Chamber Orchestra, Patrice and Renaud Fontanarosa, Marielle Nordmann, Guy Touvron, and Eric Francerie.

Although Claude Bolling expressed himself through many different styles of music, at heart he remained a jazz musician who continued to enjoy a ragtime solo, a boogie, or a Sy Oliver orchestration. Following his dream, the pianist organized a big band of highly talented musicians in the 1970s. The Claude Bolling Big Band celebrated its thirtieth anniversary in 2006, touring the world from the United States to Asia, South America, and Mexico, enjoying large audiences and much success.

Including Duke Ellington, Count Basie, Jimmy Lunceford or Glenn Miller's music, Claude Bolling's albums are a reflection of a timeless repertoire, but they also include his own compositions written in the grand tradition. He has worked with jazz personalities Joe Williams, Carmen McRae, Dee Dee Bridgewater, William "Cat" Anderson, Dizzy Gillespie, Jon Faddis, Sam Woodyard, and Rhoda Scott. Bolling performed double band performances with his own Big Band and the Duke/Mercer Ellington Orchestra, and his collaboration with Stephane Grappelli in 1991, on the album *First Class,* is one of his most successful recordings. "Bollington," as Boris Vian affectionately called him, found himself in the world of stage music, participating in the 1996 premier of *A Drum Is a Woman,* directed by Jerome Savary.

Today Claude Bolling occupies the role of itinerant musical ambassador of France throughout the world, following in the footsteps of the great French jazz musicians Django Reinhardt and Stephane Grappelli.

All the Things You Are

from *CLAUDE BOLLING TRIO – ALL TIME FAVORITES*,
a Frémeaux & Associés CD, ref. FA468 – Used by Permission

Lyrics by Oscar Hammerstein II
Music by Jerome Kern

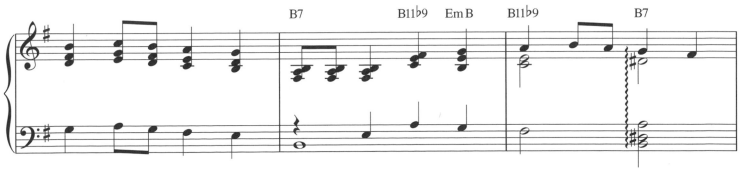

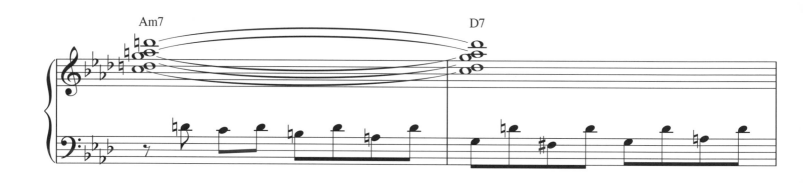

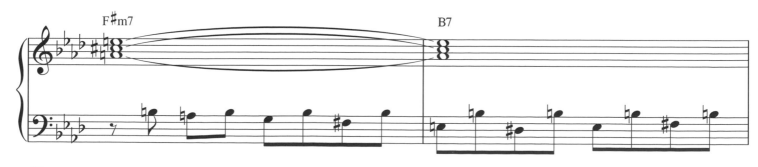

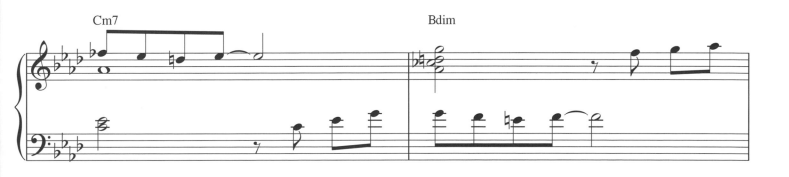

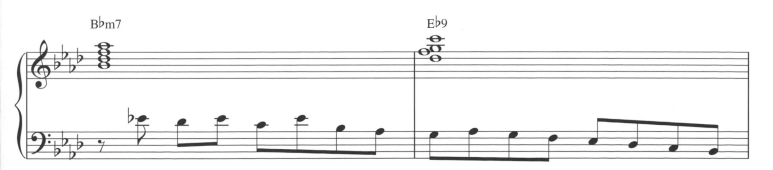

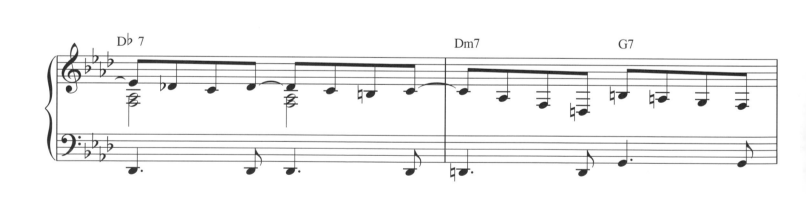

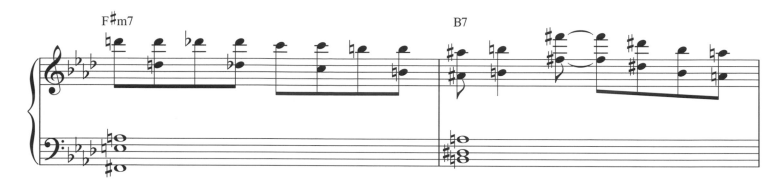

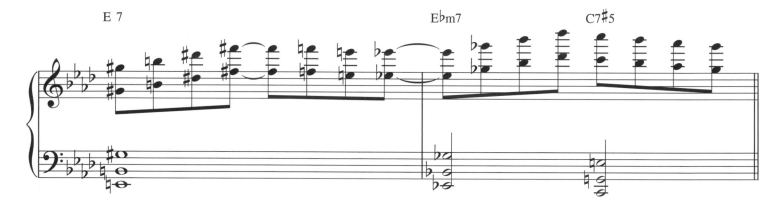

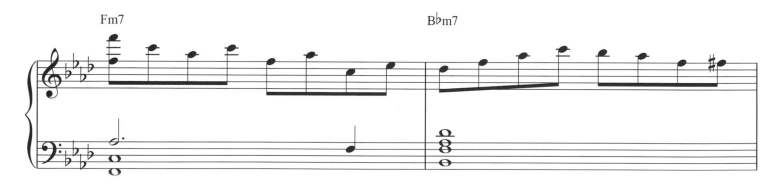

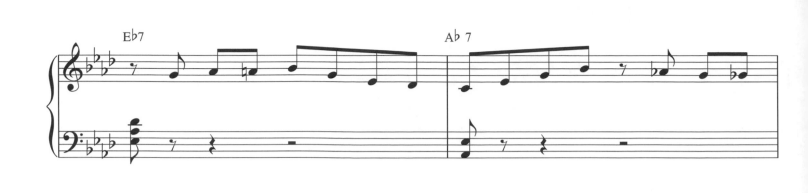

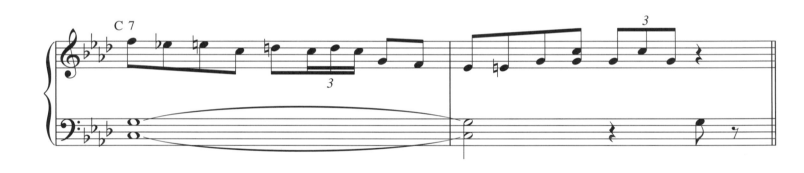

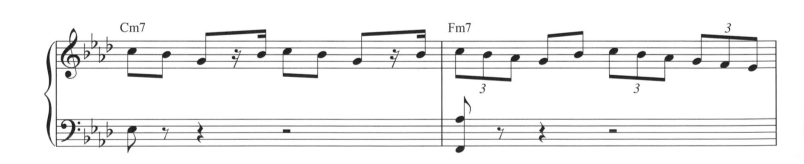

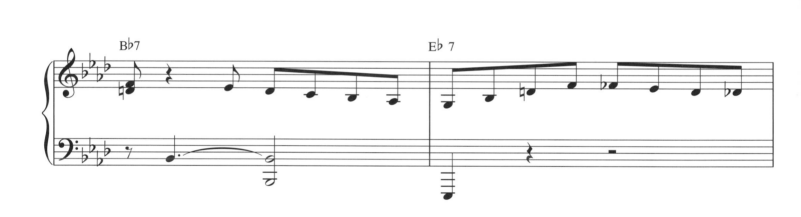

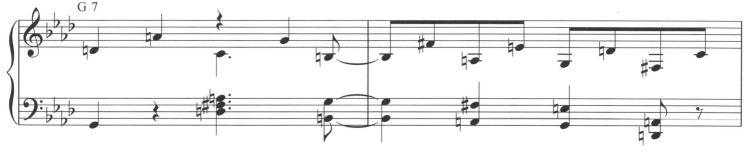

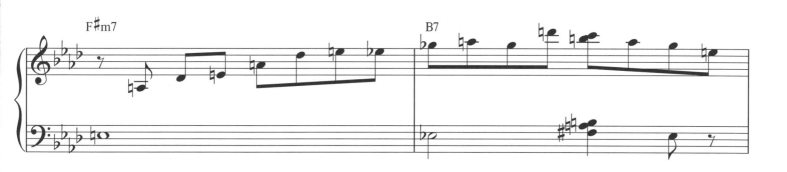

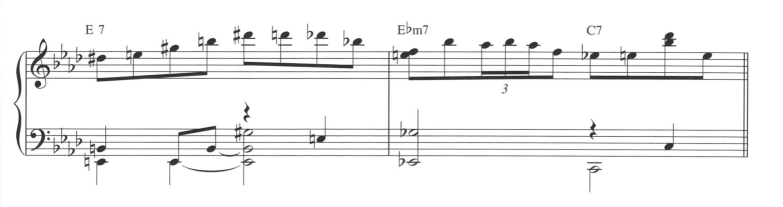

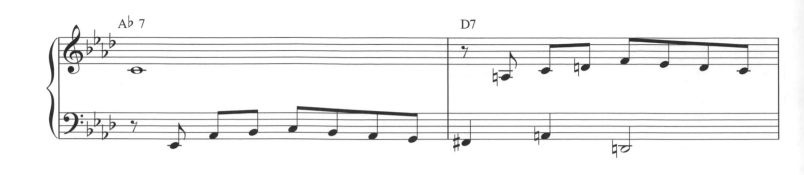

Drop Me Off in Harlem

from CLAUDE BOLLING BIG BAND – A TONE PARALLEL TO HARLEM,
a Frémeaux & Associés CD, ref. FA499 – Used by Permission

Words by Nick Kenny
Music by Duke Ellington

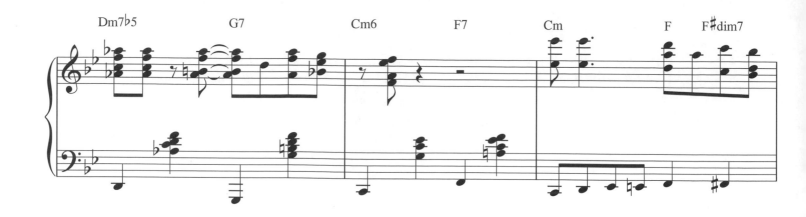

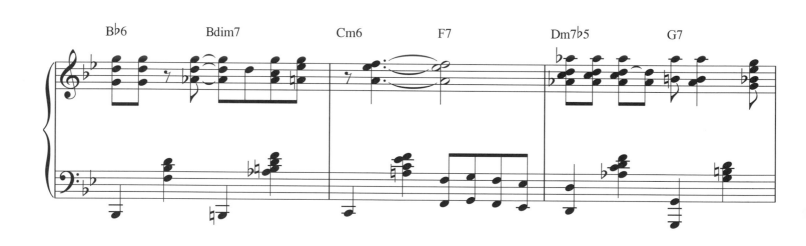

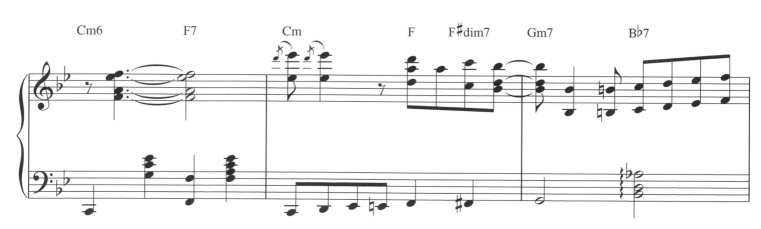

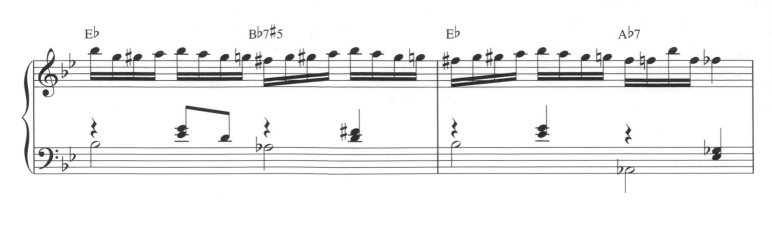

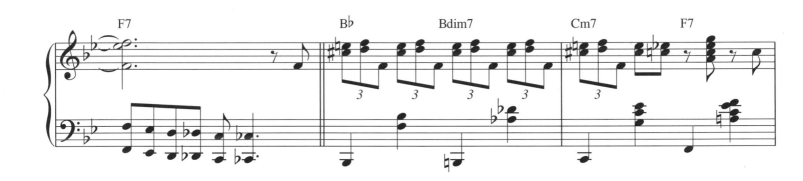

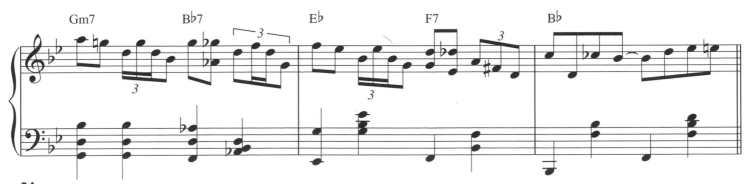

Get Happy

from CLAUDE BOLLING TRIO – ALL TIME FAVORITES,
a Frémeaux & Associés CD, ref. FA468 – Used by Permission

Lyric by Ted Koehler
Music by Harold Arlen

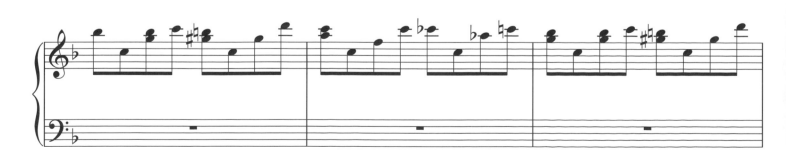

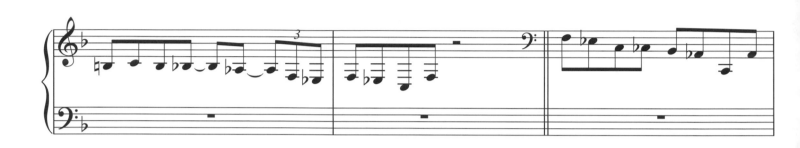

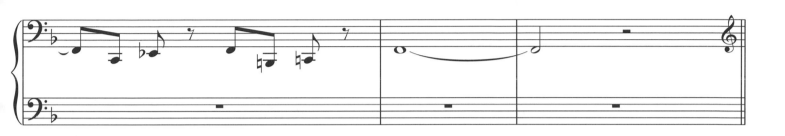

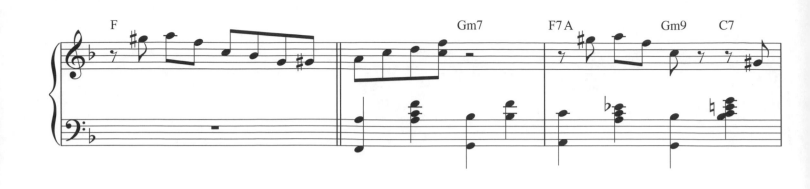

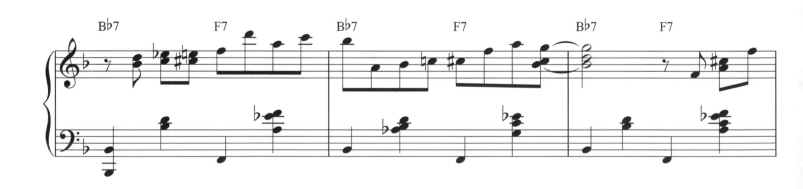

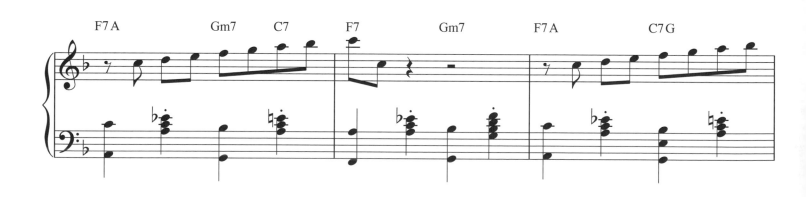

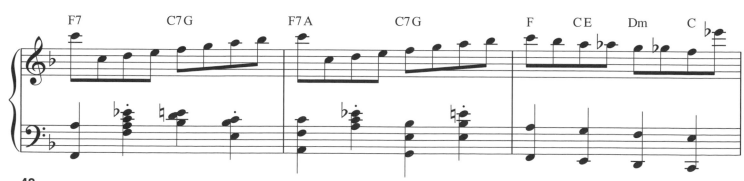

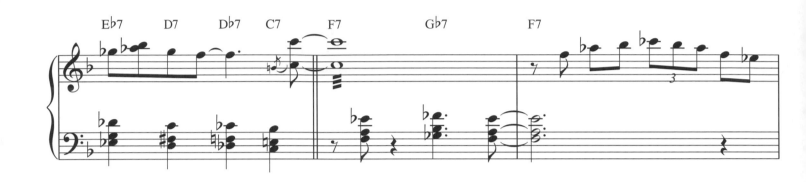

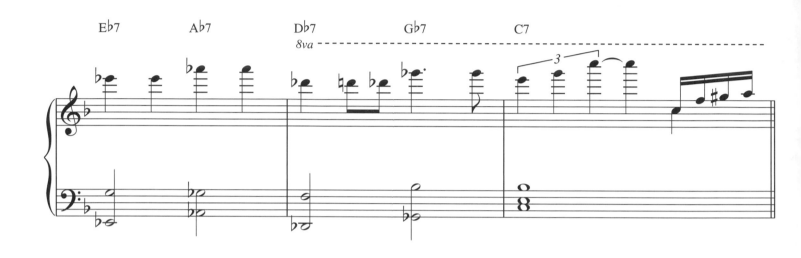

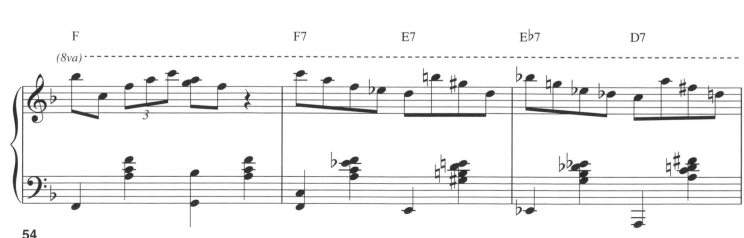

Poor Butterfly

from CLAUDE BOLLING TRIO – ALL TIME FAVORITES,
a Frémeaux & Associés CD, ref. FA468 – Used by Permission

Words by John L. Golden
Music by Raymond Hubbell

Stardust

from CLAUDE BOLLING TRIO – ALL TIME FAVORITES,
a Frémeaux & Associés CD, ref. FA468 – Used by Permission

Words by Mitchell Parish
Music by Hoagy Carmichael

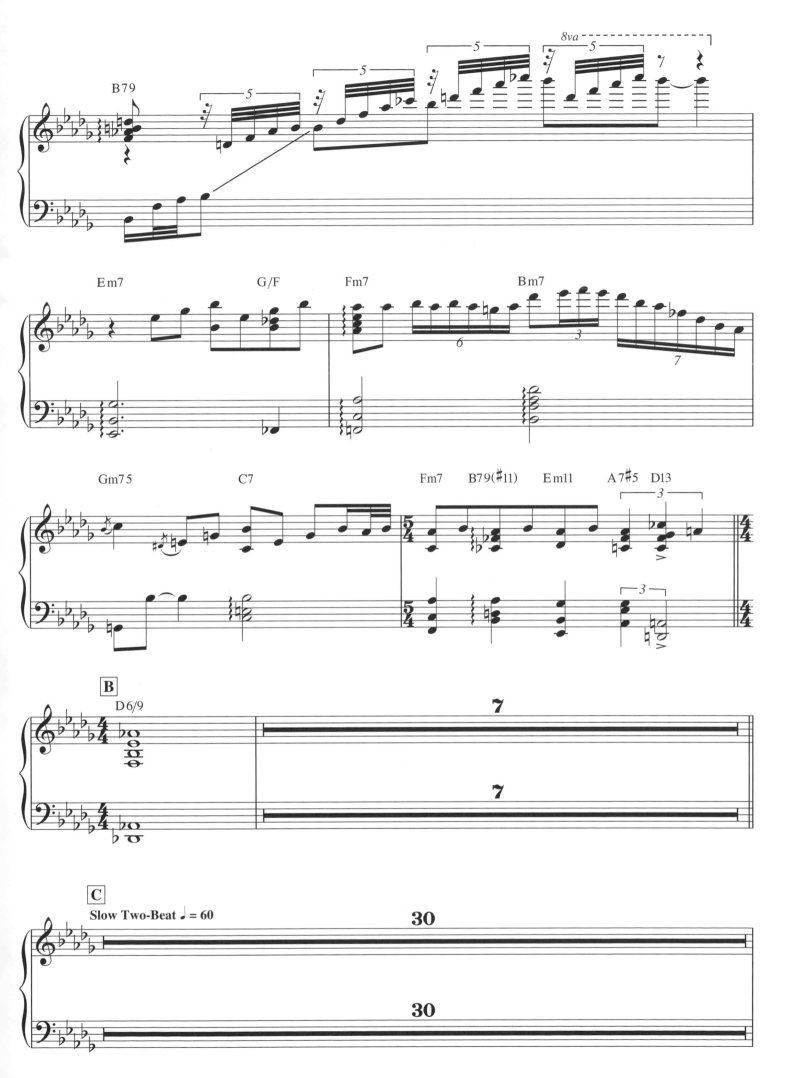

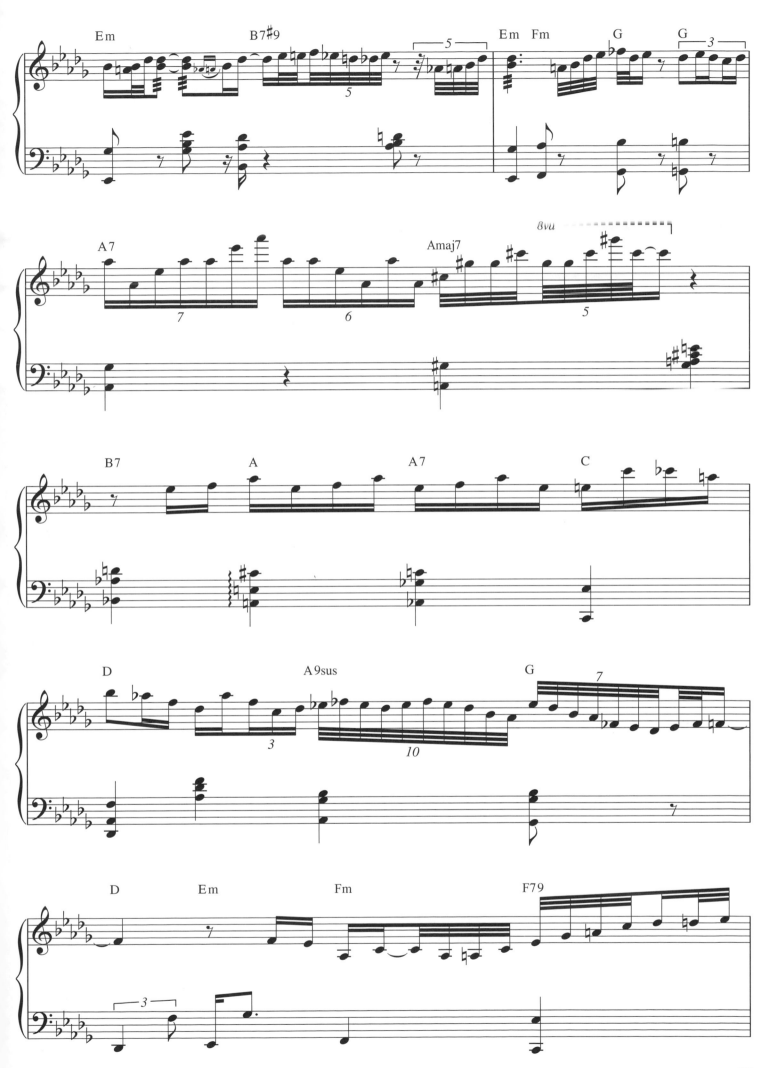

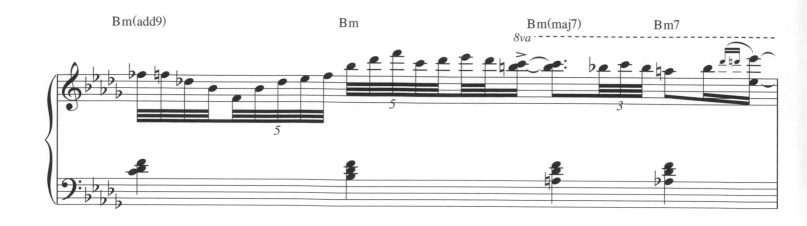

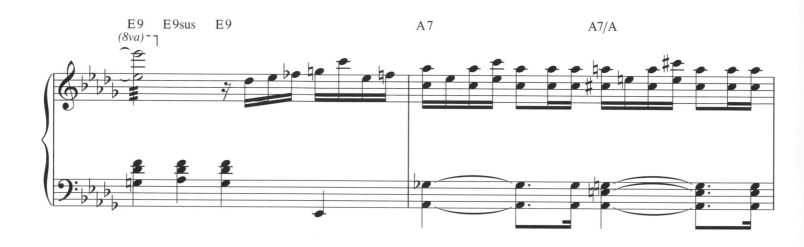

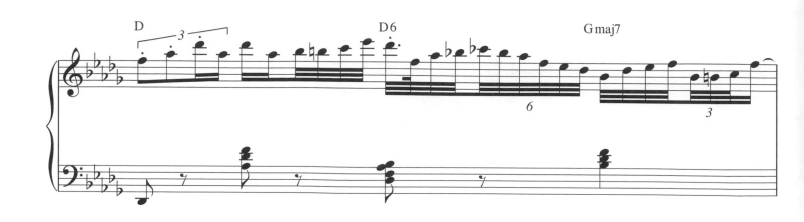

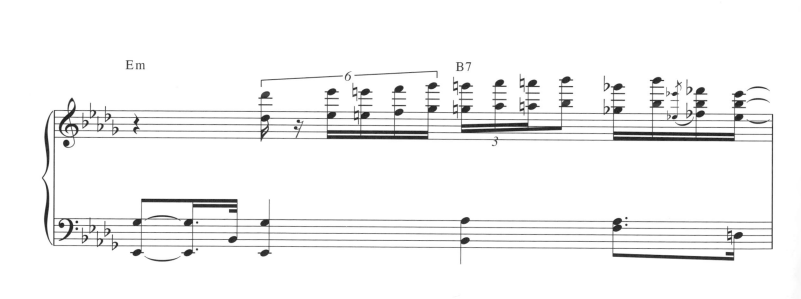

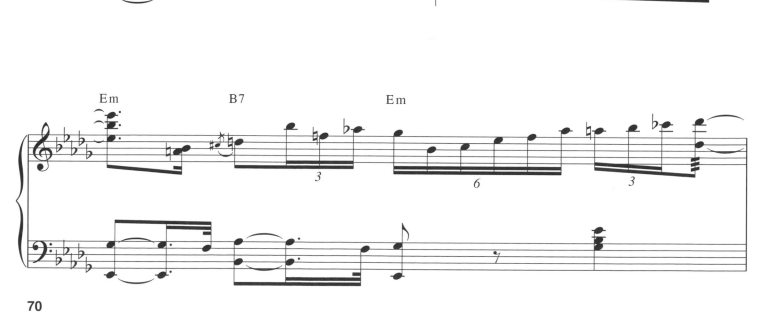

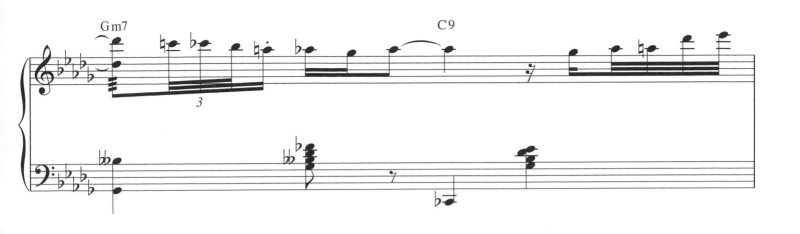

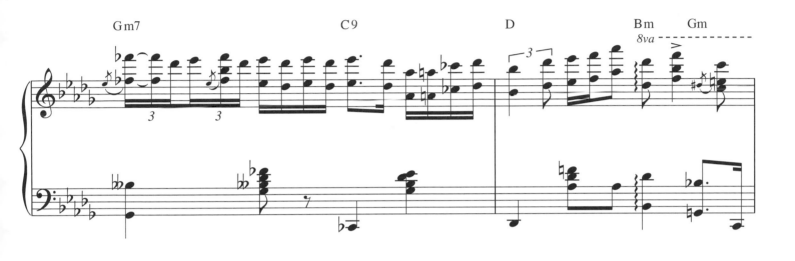

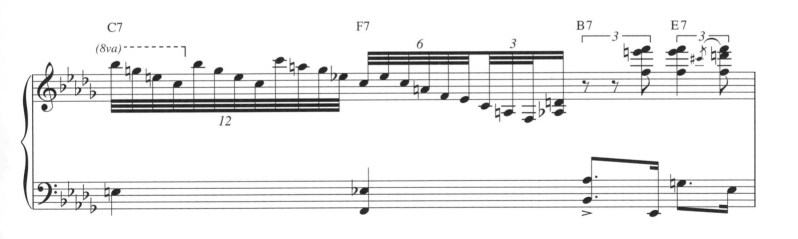

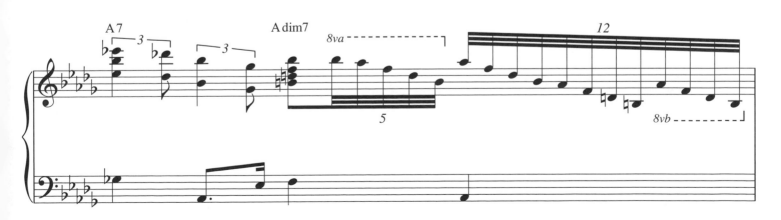